Africa's Great Rift Valley is a deep fissure in the earth's surface which came about because of what geologists call faulting, a process produced below the surface of the earth, involving the breaking of the solid rocks in its upper layers. This may be caused by them being pulled or stretched apart by tension, or squeezed together by compression.

When the forces exerted are greater than the strength of the rocks, they break along a fault. In the Rift Valley, the irresistible intensity tore the earth's crust apart at nearly parallel fault lines and between these the mass of land subsided by as much as several thousand feet to form the floor of the valley.

Below the crust of the earth, rock material normally exists in a solid state at very high temperatures and under great pressure. If the latter is reduced for any reason, the rock liquifies and combines with the water vapour present to constitute a highly explosive mixture. This forces its way up through any cracks or weakness in the earth's upper layers and explodes, causing earthquakes and volcanic eruptions. A volcano is defined as an opening in the earth's crust through which lava is expelled, forming a conical heap or, in time, a mountain many thousand feet higher than the surrounding country.

The many volcanoes in the Rift Valley are all associated with the intense volcanic activity of the last 20 million years, brought about during the formation of the extensive rift system. Although some big volcanoes – Kilimanjaro, Mounts Meru, Kenya, Elgon, and others – lie well outside the rift valleys, it is believed that their

Below: The Darter in a typical wing-drying pose.

Opposite: The Goliath Heron is the largest heron in the world, standing over 5 ft. (1.5 m.) high.

Freshwater lakes and marshes

Lake Naivasha is a freshwater lake at an altitude of 6,200 ft. (1,890 m.) in the Rift Valley, approximately 50 miles (80 km.) north-west of Nairobi and approached by an excellent tarmac road. Besides ready accessibility, it has facilities for fishing, boating, sailing and water sports. But its biggest attraction is the variety of birdlife seen on it and in its vicinity.

Not only does the lake support a miscellany of waterbirds, but many other species abound in the grasslands and acacia woodlands that surround it, making a bird count of more than 400 for the area. Lake Naivasha therefore makes an excellent illustration for this chapter. But the lake itself has another distinction which is of great interest. To bring this into perspective, it is necessary to comment upon its location, the Rift Valley.

The Kenya Rift Valley, with which we are particularly concerned, is part of the East African rift system. This extends northwards beyond the Kenya boundary to become the Ethiopian rift system. From the Afar depression the rift zone stretches past the continent of Africa into the Red Sea and through the Gulf of Aqaba, via Jordan, to end in Turkey.

In northern Kenya the Rift Valley is not very evident, but following it southwards the cleft, now about 30 miles (50 km.) wide, makes a dramatic reappearance in central and southern Kenya. Then through Tanzania's Olduvai Gorge into Lake Malawi and beyond, to terminate in Mozambique. In its entire length the Afro-Arabian rift system covers a distance of about 4,000 miles (6,500 km.).

currents, East Africa shows marked climatic differences in its three territories.

In some areas there are two well defined rainy seasons; others have only one, raining continuously from December to April. The northern parts also have only one rainy season lasting for about five months with July the wettest.

Vegetation: East Africa provides an almost complete range of habitats, from desert to savannah and from highland grasslands to montane areas. Although the main lowland rain forests exist on the wetter, western side of the continent of Africa, there are vestigial patches of Congo-type forest on the eastern side in coastal and near-coastal pockets. The scarcity of these patches of forest, and the consequent variety of their avifauna, make their preservation essential.

The non-forest zones which lie between the mountains, and the evergreen forests of the lowlands, provide a variety of localities and support the largest number of bird species. These zones include various types of savannah or grasslands, from thickish wooded savannah in the wetter areas, to drier, open, grassy country. Level low-lying plains that flood during the rainy season encourage a heavy growth of vegetation, and the breeding of numbers of weavers. Much of East Africa is made up of typical montane or highland regions, the demarcation line above which these areas are defined being at 5,000 ft. (1,500 m.) since marked changes take place both in the animal and plant populations above this height.

From harsh tracts of desert, to rolling grasslands and towering mountains, this immense and diverse area of Africa thus encompasses many types of habitat. A meeting place for vast numbers of native and immigrant birds, the region truly supports 'an abundance of birds'.

determined by a variety of factors. These include the physical structure of the landmass and its natural features; the climate and its effect on vegetation; and the presence of competitive species in areas which are otherwise suitable and easy of access. So let us look at East Africa bearing these in mind.

Physiography: The physical geography of East Africa is complicated and highly diversified, extending from sea level to high mountains. A typical continental shelf coastal plain is generally absent from the East African seaboard. Further west, immediately beyond the coastal belt, an extensive plateau rises gradually to about 3,000 ft. (900 m.) and covers a large part of northern Kenya including Wajir. To the south of Mombasa, Tanga and beyond, this zone continues as a narrow belt, but expands below Morogoro to include much of south-eastern Tanzania.

The greater part of Uganda and Tanzania, especially around Tabora and the Lake Victoria region, forms a large interior plateau varying between 2,000–6,000 ft. (600–1,800 m.). This continues in part of Kenya north-east of Moshi and Arusha through a wide fringe crossing the Athi River east of Nairobi and then running northwards as a much narrower belt.

Much of central Kenya, the northern and southern highlands of Tanzania, south-western Uganda and the Ruwenzori Mountains rise above 4,500 ft. (1,350 m.) the highest points being Kilimanjaro (19,340 ft., 5,895 m.) in Tanzania and Mount Kenya (17,058 ft., 5,200 m.). These form a distinct contrast to the surrounding lower plateaux. Finally, a number of lakes, small and large, alkaline and fresh, exist along the floor of the East African Rift Valley.

Climate: The only aspect of climate which need concern us here is the rainfall, bearing in mind its direct influence on vegetation. Because of the great range of altitudes, the wide distribution of lakes, desert and highland barriers, air movements and ocean

Introduction
An abundance of birds

Kenya is rightly proud of the great variety of its wildlife and the relative ease with which it can be seen. Animals in their natural habitat have always provided a strong attraction for visitors, but in recent years more and more travellers have become aware of the astonishing number of colourful birds found in Kenya.

The number of tourists drawn to this country by its vast and diverse avifauna is increasing yearly and it is useful to put Kenya's birdlife into a world perspective. Of an estimated 8,600 or more bird species in the world, Africa south of the Sahara can boast of about 1,750. The figure for East Africa (made up of Kenya, Uganda and Tanzania) is 1,294, and Kenya alone is represented by 1,054 species. This gives it the richest avifauna of any country on the African continent.

Keen bird-watchers who visit or live in Kenya have a chance of seeing 60 per cent of the African avifauna, and for those who can also range over Uganda and Tanzania the figure is 74 per cent. Even within a 25 mile (40 km.) radius of Nairobi, more than 50 per cent of Kenya's birds have been recorded. For an individual to see more than 100 species in a day's outing is not all that difficult, although it might be somewhat strenuous.

Kenya's bird species are only surpassed in the world by those of Columbia, Venezuela and Peru in South America where the majority, unlike those of Kenya, are forest birds and not so readily seen. The one-day record of birds counted in Kenya by an individual is 248 species. In November 1984, a team of three expert ornithologists, under strict rules and supervision, established a world record of 308 sightings in a period of 24 hours, from midnight to midnight. Both records indicate the excellent visibility of bird varieties in this country.

So what makes East Africa, and particularly Kenya, so special? From a global point of view, geographical distribution of species is

Preface

This is *not* a field guide to the birds of Kenya. Its main purpose is to illustrate some of the commoner and more colourful birds which cannot fail to attract visitors and others who travel round the country to various towns, national parks, lakes and the coast. It tells you where you are likely to see them and interesting facts about them. For the keener birdwatcher, other works are available.

The division of birds into their habitats is somewhat arbitrary and used as a convenient device. It is true that birds which live in evergreen forests are not, with a few exceptions, found in non-forest areas. Similarly, few species seen at high altitudes frequent low-lying plains. But quite a number of birds, not confined to such specialized areas, may well be seen in more than one of the described habitats.

Birds living in highland and rain forests are rarely visible to casual watchers. The same applies to those whose habitats are on mountains and inland cliffs. Therefore these are generally considered outside the scope of this publication.

Classification, scientific names, and rarely, common names of birds tend to change in time as more facts about them become known by ornithologists. The latest information for East Africa is in *Birds of East Africa, their habitat, status and distribution*, edited by P. L. Britton and published in Nairobi in 1980 by the East African Natural History Society.

The writing of *Beautiful Birds of Kenya* has been somewhat demanding as a tight deadline had to be met, but my task has been made considerably easier by the whole-hearted co-operation of the producer, Mohamed Amin, and the devoted support of the two text editors, my wife Joan and daughter Shereen. To all three I express my sincere appreciation. My grateful thanks also to Sally Johansson who, through her efficiency and expertise, made the production of the typescript painless.

Note: *Birds whose names appear in* **bold type** *in the text are illustrated in the book. Refer to the bird index on pages 121 and 123.*

Previous page: Lake Bogoria is another site which occasionally provides a mass of flamingos as a feast for the eyes.

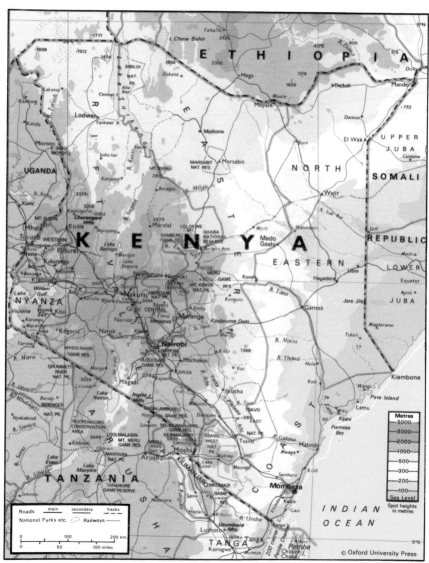

Contents

For Kainde, our dear granddaughter

This edition published 1993 by
Text Book Centre Ltd.
Kijabe Street,
P.O. Box 47540
Nairobi
Kenya

First published 1985

Second Impression 1989
Third Impression 1993

ISBN 1 874041 31 8

Designed and produced by
Camerapix Publishers International
P.O. Box 45048, Nairobi, Kenya

Text edited by Joan Karmali and Shereen Karmali
Designed by Craig Dodd
Printed in Hong Kong by South China Printing Co.

Half-title: The Greater Cormorant, which exists entirely on fish and catches its prey with great efficiency. Title page: A flock of Cattle Egrets take off near Lake Jipe. Contents page: Early morning sunshine on Lake Naivasha with an array of Greater Cormorants on a mud island.

Beautiful
BIRDS *of* KENYA

John Karmali

Text Book Centre

origin is due to the working of the same forces that formed the rift system, and coincides with its creation.

Not only do lakes have their origin in mountains, their composition is also determined by them. Rain washing down or seeping through a mountainside emerges, at a lower level, as a river or a spring. By then the water is chemically very different from the original rain, having absorbed various substances during its passage.

Although lava can be acid or basic, most of those in East Africa tend to be the latter. As a result water flowing from a volcanic mountain contains alkaline salts dissolved in it. And its contents become even more concentrated when it reaches a lake and is subject to evaporation.

From this, it would be reasonable to assume all lakes in the rift would be alkaline. So let us consider the lakes in the Kenya Rift Valley. Starting with Lake Magadi in the south and travelling northward, we have Lakes Naivasha, Elementeita, Nakuru, Bogoria, Baringo and Turkana, the last being on the border of Ethiopia. Of these, Naivasha and Baringo are in fact *freshwater* lakes, all the others being alkaline, with Magadi having the greatest concentration of salts.

Both Naivasha and Baringo are fed by streams flowing from the same type of volcanic catchment areas as the other five, but despite that continue to be fresh. To remain so, a lake must have an outlet to flush away the alkaline salts and so prevent their concentration. Yet, in both cases there are no obvious rivers visibly draining the

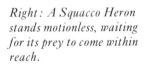

Above: The Hadada Ibis is a gregarious bird, often associated with river valleys in towns, and has a loud raucous cry.

Right: A Squacco Heron stands motionless, waiting for its prey to come within reach.

Opposite: The Black-headed Heron has diversified its eating habits to forage for food both in water and on land.

contents of these lakes. J. W. Gregory, who pioneered research in the geology of the Rift Valley in the 1890s, had a possible answer. According to him, Lake Baringo used to be drained in ancient times by a large river at its northern end. Volcanic upheavals in due course blocked this outlet, but Gregory believed that this essential seepage still remained in the same area, but went underground and became invisible. There are no signs of any such subterranean exits near the lake today, but Gregory's explanation seems to have some substance.

Similarly it is possible Lake Naivasha also has an identical leak on the south side, opposite the two rivers which flow into it from the north.

There are two significant differences in the life on alkaline and freshwater lakes. The former support no vegetation growth, except some algae, while the latter have plants flourishing in the water around their shores. Even more meaningful from our point of interest, freshwater lakes nourish abundant fish fauna, whereas the alkaline ones contain either no fish or only a few specialized species. Lake Turkana, being less alkaline, is an exception. The presence of all this freshwater fish, some of it close inshore, supports an enormous number of fish-eating birds. And these are the species we shall mainly concentrate on in this chapter. Besides Naivasha and Baringo, other accessible freshwater habitats are Lake Jipe in Tsavo West and the extensive swamps in Amboseli National Park.

It is appropriate to mention here the wide, slow-moving rivers in Kenya such as the Tana which also attract the birds which make fish their main diet. But their special attraction and value for avifauna are the luxuriant forests which fringe their banks.

A visitor to any freshwater lake will most probably see some largish birds, mainly black, perched on rocks, logs or tree branches near water, generally with their wings outstretched. These are cormorants of which there are two species in Kenya. The larger one, the **Greater Cormorant**, is 36 in. (90 cm.) long and is black, with white on the foreneck and breast, whereas the smaller Long-tailed Cormorant is entirely black. They fish below the surface of the water, diving and swimming in pursuit of their prey. The catch is normally brought to the surface, tossed in the air, and then swallowed. The bird, back on a perch, carries out the typical drying movement of the waterbird – by wing flapping and body shaking – after which it holds out its wings for a long time to complete the process.

The **African Darter** looks like an elongated cormorant and is similar in its habits of catching a fish or drying its wings. But it is readily distinguished from the cormorant by its much longer neck, which assumes an S-shape when at rest, and only its underparts are completely black. The elongated neck has a specialized structure which works like a trigger enabling the bird to shoot its bill forward to spear the fish.

Other eye-catching large-sized fishing birds are herons, ibises and storks, which fish while standing still or wading in the water, not far from the shore. Of them the most obvious is the **Goliath Heron**. Standing about 60 in. (150 cm.) high, it has the distinction

Above: The White-faced Whistling Duck with its young family on a floating grass island in Amboseli.

Left: Regarded as sacred and kept in captivity by the ancient Egyptians, the Egyptian Goose has a strident honking call.

Above: When the light is right, the iridescence of its wings makes the large Spur-winged Goose even more attractive.

Right: The male Knob-billed Goose with its characteristic 'knob' developed during the breeding season.

23

of being the largest of all herons. The **Black-headed Heron** is considerably smaller being 38 in. (95 cm) in size, and is readily distinguished by its grey, white and black colouration. Besides its aquatic life it has taken to the land where it can be observed, a considerable distance from water, feeding on insects and rats.

An even smaller heron, worth looking for because it demonstrates the characteristically stealthy fishing technique of the heron family, is the **Squacco Heron**. Rather thickset, it has a rich, biscuit-coloured body and white wings during the breeding season. When searching for food, the bird stands absolutely still, its neck usually retracted, waiting for prey to come within striking distance, when it is caught with astounding rapidity. Very occasionally herons, while standing still and sighting their prey, move their heads laterally from side to side, obviously to obtain binocular fixation before striking.

A special characteristic of ibises is the downcurved bill. Of them, the **Hadada Ibis** is distinguished by having perhaps the most raucous cry of any bird of its size, which it uses to announce its presence at sunset and sunrise, and even on bright moonlit nights. It is a gregarious bird, 30 in. (75 cm.) in size, and generally looks quite drab with its mostly olive-brown feathers, until suddenly it shows an attractive flash of metallic green irridescence on its wings when the light is right. The more commonly seen **Sacred Ibis** is mentioned in more detail in Chapter 3.

As is to be expected, freshwater lakes provide a suitable home for a variety of ducks, some resident and others migrant. They vary greatly in size, the largest being the **Spurwing Goose**. Despite its size, it is not a goose but a species of tree duck. Its length of 36 in (90 cm.), dark-red bill, glossy metallic black upper parts, and white belly, make it easy to identify. A much smaller tree duck, only about half the size of the above, is the **White-faced Whistling Duck** and, as its name suggests, its call is a loud clear whistle, usually repeated several times. It is readily distinguished, with its white face, generally rufous plumage, and barred flanks, and is seen fairly frequently.

Ducks and geese pass through a flightless period of some weeks after the breeding season, which makes them especially vulnerable to predators. All the flight feathers moult simultaneously, quite unlike other birds, which shed them one after the other and so can continue to fly.

The **Egyptian Goose** is very common in East Africa. It has a predominantly brown plumage with white shoulders and is 24 in. (60 cm.) long. Its honking call is readily recognizable. The Egyptians regarded these birds as sacred and often depicted them on murals in the tombs of their ancestors. Another similar sized goose, but nearly silent, is the **Knob-billed Goose** readily identifiable because of its black and white feathers, the black upper part showing a metallic sheen. The male of this species develops a striking looking knob at the base of the bill during the breeding season.

With its black velvety crown, distinctive straw-coloured crest, bare cheeks and red neck-wattle, the **Crowned Crane** may well be

Above: The Crowned Crane is the national bird of Uganda, but found commonly all over Africa.

Right: The Pied Kingfisher, with its black and white plumage, is readily recognized by its technique of hovering over water to fish.

Opposite: The Fish Eagle, as its name implies, feeds exclusively on fish.

27

described as one of the most beautiful of the larger African birds. It is about 40 in. (100 cm.) in size. A pair of cranes, or even more, perform a ceremonial dance fascinating to watch. The birds open their wings wide, bow stiffly to each other and then suddenly leap two or three feet in the air, coming down to run around each other and start the ritual all over again.

Of the three birds of prey characteristic of lake shores, the most common is the **Fish Eagle**. Its plumage is striking – white head, chest, back and tail, chestnut belly, and black wings. It generally sits prominently on a tall tree near water to spy for fish. Another conspicuous feature is its call, so dramatically distinctive that it haunts the memory for ever. It catches fish on the surface with consummate ease, and these provide 90 per cent of its diet.

Another flyer seen close to the shores is the tiny jewel-like **Malachite Kingfisher**. Less than 6 in. (15 cm.) long, it flashes among reeds, sometimes using them as a perch as it looks for prey, mostly fish but not exclusively so. At Lake Naivasha its main diet seems to be tree frogs. With its cobalt-blue crown barred with black, upper parts bright ultramarine blue, and underparts rufous, this exquisite little bird is a true gem. In sharp contrast, the somewhat sober, black-and-white **Pied Kingfisher** can also be seen, mostly hovering over the water. (Also see Chapter 3).

All waters attract a variety of gulls. A species which confines itself almost exclusively to large inland lakes is the **Grey-headed Gull**. It has the typical general appearance of its family and is largely white and pale grey, with a conspicuous grey head, and red bill and legs. Gulls fly over water and alight on it to catch fish.

Turning to small species which haunt water, one can often see a thickset bird, with nondescript blackish-slate colouring and a red knob on its forehead, in considerable numbers. This is the **Red-knobbed Coot**, 16 in. (40 cm.) long. They feed mainly on sub-surface vegetation, and their constant browsing helps keep the water free of weed. Sportsmen believe, without proof, that coots compete with wild duck, and consequently thousands have been shot wantonly at Lake Naivasha. Fishermen, who also seem to detest them, might well reflect that without the coots it would hardly be possible to drive a boat or cast a lure through the weed.

African Jacana, also known as Lily-trotters, are curious long-legged birds, with very extended toes. Their widespread feet enable them to walk and feed on water-lily leaves and other floating aquatic vegetation. Once they were plentiful at Lake Naivasha, but sadly no longer since the accidental and unfortunate introduction of the Coypu, a beaver-like mammal, into the lake. The intruders found a diet of aquatic plants, especially waterlilies, very much to their taste with the inevitable result that these have almost completely disappeared, and consequently so have the Jacana.

Above: The Grey-headed Gull is somewhat unusual in that it prefers inland to coastal waters.

Left: Note the strangely long toes of the Jacana, enabling it to spread its weight and so walk on aquatic plants.

Above: The unfortunate Red-knobbed Coot was wrongly regarded by sportsmen as competing with wild duck, and so shot in its thousands in recent years. It is now protected.

Right: The beautiful Malachite Kingfisher will eat tree-frogs and other amphibians as well as fish.

Alkaline lakes

Lakes with a high alkaline content are a special feature of Africa's rift system. The Kenya Rift Valley has five such lakes. Beginning in the south and going north, they are Magadi, Elmenteita, Nakuru, Bogoria and Turkana. All have their own distinctive character and are worth looking at briefly.

Lake Magadi, the most alkaline, is about 40 sq. miles (104 sq. km.) in area at an altitude of 1,900 ft. (580 m.). It looks rather like a scene out of hell, with the enormous growth of crystalline soda on its surface, appearing a coconut-icing pink from a distance. The mirages shimmer in the stupefying heat and visitors should take a plentiful supply of water and some salt tablets to prevent serious dehydration.

The smallest, Lake Elmenteita, is only 7 sq. miles (18 sq. km.) in size and located at about 5,900 ft. (1,800 m.) in a lunar-like landscape made up of lava outflows and volcanic craters. From there one has to travel only 25 miles (40 km.) and drop 100 ft. (30 m.) or so to reach Lake Nakuru. Being seasonal, its surface area fluctuates between 2 sq. miles (5 sq. km.) and 12 sq. miles (30 sq. km.). At its lowest, it is a dismal expanse of smelly mud, with barely any life, but when full it is a nutritious green soup with plentiful activity in and around it.

One drops to 3,200 ft. (975 m.) on reaching Lake Bogoria. Somewhat less than twice the size of Elmenteita, it is set in a broad basin at the base of a 2,000 ft. (600 m.) mountain wall, with active steam jets on its foreshore. The countryside around is hot, dry and dusty, and is uninviting with its scrub and thornbush.

Farthest north at 1,800 ft. (550 m.) lies Lake Turkana, its northern shore just across the border into Ethiopia. With its vast area of 2,470 sq. miles (6,400 sq. km.), it is the largest alkaline lake in the world. Compared to the other four, however, it is much less alkaline and the concentration of salts in it is well within the limits that allow life to thrive. Hence a variety of fish live in it and, as a consequence, the birds which prey on them also flourish. This hospitable situation exists because of the steady flow of fresh water into the lake from the River Omo in the north. Water lost by evaporation is replaced by the incoming stream and the favourable balance is maintained.

Alkaline lakes have no outlets, either through subterranean springs or overland rivers, to flush away the inflowing chemicals. The alkalinity consists mainly of sodium carbonate and its compounds, derived from the drainage of basic lava rocks, in turn the result of volcanic upheavals. The salts flow into the closed lakes and are concentrated by evaporation. (Also see Chapter 1). In the case of Lake Magadi the waters coming into it from thermal springs are already strongly alkaline, and with the hot sun causing rapid evaporation, and little rainfall to replace the moisture lost, the mass of salt is continuously crystallized.

It has already been mentioned that compared to the profusion and variety of life, including fish, nourished by freshwater lakes, alkaline ones support hardly any. This does not mean that they support no life at all. Specialized forms which have adapted to this hostile environment do exist and even prosper in the harsh

conditions. One special example is the small fish *Tilapia grahami*. This little creature has been responsible for a remarkable ecological upheaval in recent years, but more about this later.

To every visitor who comes to Kenya, the mention of Lake Nakuru immediately conjures up the spectacle of pink flamingos in vast numbers. But how many people realize that the existence of this fantastic sight depends entirely on the fact that it is an *alkaline* lake? The flamingo story is fascinating and well worth telling.

Authorities vary in their opinion, and divide the flamingo family into four to six species. We are concerned with only two, the Lesser and the Greater Flamingo. It has been estimated that there are over 6·5 million flamingos in the world. The **Lesser Flamingo** is the most numerous, about 5.5 million of them being distributed over Africa, India and the Persian Gulf. The great majority, approximately 4 million, live in the foul alkaline lakes on the floor of the East African Rift Valley.

The **Greater Flamingo** are much smaller in concentration, being outnumbered by nearly a hundred to one by the Lesser. They can be seen stalking alongside the latter, easily distinguished by their spectacular height. It is hardly necessary to describe the flamingos in detail except to point out that the male Greater Flamingo can tower to a height of 6 ft. (1.8 m.) whereas the Lesser Flamingo, which is the smallest of the family, is only 3 ft. (0.9 m.) high. In each case the female is smaller than the male. Both species are pink, have red legs with webbed feet, a long sinuous neck and a large bill, the latter being deep carmine-red in the Lesser.

The unique feature of the flamingo is its bill, especially adapted for its highly individual style of food intake. The lower mandible is large and boat-shaped, the upper, being smaller, fits on it like a lid; and in the groove between lies the tongue. The inside lining of the mouth cavity, consisting of combined scales with an edging of stiff hair, make the bill a very efficient filter. The water with its suspension of fine food particles is sucked in by the piston-like retraction of the tongue. Its forward movement then forces out only the water, leaving the food behind to be swallowed.

The Greater Flamingo has an additional filtering refinement which enables it to feed on larger organisms such as molluscs and crustacea in addition to the much smaller algae and diatoms. On the other hand the diet of the Lesser Flamingo is confined almost exclusively to the last two items. Their effective feeding method means that the floating particles are filtered out almost dry. Little if any alkaline water, which could prove fatal, is swallowed. Flamingos prefer to drink less saline water and regularly frequent springs or freshwater inlets to supply this need.

Flamingos visit the alkaline lakes of the Rift Valley in large numbers, often well exceeding a million, making a fantastic spectacle. The amount of nourishment, mainly algae and diatoms, taken out of the waters of the alkaline lakes by their astronomical numbers is staggering. According to Brown (1973), the intake of a million Lesser Flamingos is 180 tons (183 tonne) daily, or over 65,000 tons (66,040 tonne) a year!

Obviously an abundant supply of algae, especially the blue-

Left: The Marabou Stork is now more of a scavenger than a waterbird, and is often seen near city refuse dumps.

*Bottom left : Its specially
evolved bill and method of
feeding by filtration
enables the Lesser
Flamingo to feed on
microscopic algae.*

*Below : The great pink mass of Lesser Flamingo makes
a spectacular and unforgettable sight.*

green algae *Spirulina platensis*, is essential for the well-being of the Lesser Flamingo. Research carried out over the years indicates that conductivity and alkalinity (due to the high concentration of carbonates) combined with relatively warm temperatures, the droppings of millions of birds, and sunlight provide ideal conditions for the algae's profuse growth. Weather conditions affect the lake level, and so influence the concentration of salts. These fluctuations should in turn inhibit or encourage production of the blue-green algae, but this has not been proved.

An adequate supply of food, however, does not appear the only factor influencing the presence or absence of flamingos. Enormous variations in number take place on these lakes, birds leaving a particular one, even when the blue-green algae is obviously present. A great deal more research on the lakes is needed to get a complete answer.

Besides the flamingo, Lake Nakuru has another claim to biological distinction – the presence of the **White Pelican** in, for them, very substantial numbers. To appreciate the significance of this, we have to look back at the recent breeding behaviour of this bird.

There is no record of pelicans breeding in Kenya before 1968. This could be because no lake in the Kenya Rift Valley had enough fish to meet the enormous demands of a breeding colony of pelicans. Their intake at this time is prodigious. It is estimated a breeding adult needs 2.5 pounds (1,130 gm.) of fish a day.

Their main breeding grounds were Lake Shala in Ethiopia and

Lake Rukwa in Tanzania. Brown and Urban carried out an exhaustive study of the colonies at the former site in the 1960s. One startling fact which emerged was that Lake Shala, in which the volcanic Pelican Island breeding settlement was situated, had practically no fish. So where did the necessary immense food supply come from? A full colony of 5,000 birds at this stage would need well over 5 tons (5 tonne) a day.

Careful observation gave the answer. Shala provided the secure, undisturbed and isolated nesting area needed by these highly sensitive and touchy birds. To obtain fish, birds took off from the island, found the thermals which spiralled and lifted them over the intervening 3,000 ft. (900 m.) high ridge to the north and, having overcome this obstacle, glided down to the well-stocked Lake Abiata 10 miles (16 km.) on the other side. The return journey was made the next day. As the morning sun warmed the ground on both sides of the mountain and established the necessary upward movement of hot air currents, a two-way traffic began and continued daily until the young birds matured and left.

Now this is where the remarkable little fish *Tilapia grahami* mentioned earlier comes in. One of the special forms of animal life which has adapted over many thousands of years, it not only survives but thrives in waters so alkaline they would kill most fish. This tiny creature, about 2–3 in. (5–7.5 cm.) in size, originally only lived in the warm alkaline springs that run into Lake Magadi. When subjected to a temperature much above 100°F (38°C) it dies but, strangely enough, when placed in fresh cool water, it flourishes

41

and increases to 6–8 in. (15–20 cm.).

In 1960–1 the fish was introduced into Lake Nakuru by the health authorities to combat, by eating their larvae, the mosquitos which bred around the lake shore. After an initial failure, the *Tilapia grahami* liked its new environment, grew in size, multiplied enormously, and soon colonized the whole lake. The ecological effect of this breeding success was striking. Since 1961 Lake Nakuru has supported a large resident population of many species of fish-eating birds.

Lake Nakuru had always been a staging post for pelicans, coming down to rest during their migratory movements. Now, rather dramatically, it provided a ready and substantial food supply. In theory, breeding could take place. But where was the safe, inviolate location for a colony? The presence of Greater Flamingo breeding in 1968 at nearby Lake Elmenteita provided the incentive, and triggered off the nesting. The insecure, threatened flamingos were chased off the sheltered lava islands in Elmenteita, the White Pelican took over and 7,000–8,000 pairs of them bred successfully from 1968–71. They returned in 1973 and again in 1975. But Lake Elmenteita, being alkaline, has no fish. So the pelicans flew the 10 miles (16 km.) or so, over the hills in between, to feed at Nakuru thus, curiously, following the same pattern as that between Lakes Shala and Abieta in Ethiopia.

It is probable the pelicans seen in such large numbers at Lake Nakuru are a mixture of migrants and a new resident population bred at Elmenteita. How prolific a supply of *Tilapia grahami* Lake

Nakuru provides is indicated by the calculation that, if 1,000 pelicans eat over 1 ton (1 tonne) of fish daily, then an average population of 6,000–8,000 would consume 2,500–3,300 tons (2,540–3,350 tonne) of fish a year!

The White Pelican, over 60 in. (150 cm.) long and with a wing span of about 120 in. (300 cm.), is almost entirely white with black flight feathers. One often sees it in association with another species, the Pink-backed Pelican, distinguished by its smaller size, pale grey plumage and a head crest.

Now to look at some of the other birds of the alkaline lakes, again with emphasis on Lake Nakuru, a favourite venue for most visitors.

Pelicans and flamingos may well be the most obvious, but there are a number of other attractive smaller species. The **Avocet** is readily recognized by its contrasting black and white plumage, lengthy upturned bill, and long grey-blue legs. As it walks through shallow water, with its bill slightly open, the bird sweeps it from side to side, sifting out the food, which consists of aquatic insects, small molluscs and crustaceae. Avocet reside in Kenya in small numbers, but come the European winter, they are augmented by thousands of migrants escaping the bitter northern weather.

Another black-and-white species, this time with a straight long bill, and extraordinary vermilion-red legs, cannot fail to catch the eye. This is the **Black-winged Stilt**. Its limbs are longer in proportion to its body than all other birds with the exception of the flamingo. It is 15 in. (37.5 cm.) long and its diet is much like that of the avocet. When disturbed at nest, the parents demonstrate their

Left : The Blacksmith Plover gets its name from the similarity of its call to the sound of a hammer hitting an anvil.

Opposite : The Avocet population seen in Kenya during the northern winter consists mostly of migrants, though a small proportion is resident.

Left : The Ruff seems to favour Lake Nakuru as its wintering ground where it is often seen in its thousands.

Right: The elegant Black-winged Stilt walks in shallow pools along lake shores, probing for food with its elongated pointed bill.

47

adeptness at diversion, as they walk away dragging an open wing on the ground as if it were damaged. (See Crowned Plover in Chapter 6.)

Two species of storks are also readily observed. The **Yellow-billed Stork** has black and pinkish-white plumage, red legs and an orange, slightly down-curved bill. It is said to have fast reflexes and consequently can catch fish and frogs with astounding rapidity and ease while standing in the water, its open bill half-submerged.

The **Marabou Stork** is far from handsome, but its ugly appearance has the advantage of making it readily recognizable. It is perhaps the most common stork in Africa and is often associated with towns and villages because of its scavenging habits. It still maintains its aquatic nature to a certain extent, and at Lake Nakuru it has developed the gruesome technique of catching flamingo chicks by stampeding a flock and picking up a straggler.

A number of waders and plovers, mostly migrants (see also Chapter 3), are often seen in their thousands at Nakuru. By far the most numerous of these is the **Ruff**. Fourteen birds ringed in the Kenya Rift Valley have been recovered in the USSR and one can assume that these migrants come mainly from that area. It is a pity they are in their non-breeding plumage when in Kenya as this bird is very spectacular and elegant in full breeding array. They are rarely seen at the coast.

The **Blacksmith Plover** is not a migrant but a resident. It occurs commonly inland near water where short grass and muddy shores are present. It is about 11 in. (27.5 cm.) long and has distinctive black, white and grey plumage, its white crown being very obvious. This plover is normally silent but becomes very aggressive and noisy during breeding time. The bird flies repeatedly and fearlessly at the enemy, dive-bombing and uttering its characteristic metallic cry suggestive of a hammer hitting an anvil, from which it derives its name.

As a general rule birds which rely on water for their food supply will favour most of the aquatic habitats in Kenya which supply their need, and therefore a number of birds mentioned in the first three chapters are sometimes seen in any of these locations. You are therefore advised to consider these chapters jointly.

Below: The Great White Egret is almost completely white, with black legs.

Below: The Sacred Ibis, revered by the ancient Egyptians, no longer exists in that country.

Coastal areas

Mention of the Kenya coast conjures up memorable visions of miles and miles of white sandy coastline running north and south of Mombasa. The waters of the Indian Ocean rise and fall regularly every twelve hours or so covering most of the foreshore at high tide and, during its ebb, exposing large areas of the seashore with its old coral reefs surrounded by dazzling sand.

Visitors to Kenya escaping the northern winter, will be attracted during their walk along the beach by sizeable mixed parties of wading birds running in and out with the tide, foraging for food on the water's edge. Other birds can be seen searching and probing in the rock pools. They are mostly waders and plovers, who have emulated the tourist and migrated from their northern breeding areas, now inhospitable, to a warmer climate.

Migration, in its strict sense, means a one-way journey. It implies there is no return. A man leaves one country and migrates to another to make his home there. But birds are different. Because they have wings, an extraordinary ability to navigate, and astounding stamina, they fly not only away, but back – a round trip in fact. So bird migration signifies a series of movements. They inhabit two alternate areas, one in which to breed and the other more fitted for survival when the breeding area becomes climatically inhospitable.

A good breeding area must fulfil certain conditions for the successful reproduction of the species. It should provide appropriate nesting sites and an abundant food supply with which to feed the growing and demanding young. And long daylight hours are necessary in which to collect this food. This condition obtains in the higher latitudes. So spring is the season for breeding in the Northern Hemisphere. Come autumn, the birds travel southwards.

Why birds migrate now becomes clear. The majority of those from the northern areas fly long distances deep into Africa to escape winter conditions in the north, where the larger land masses are covered in snow and ice. These are the species that perform what are called 'distant' migrations, covering many hundreds to thousands of miles.

So-called 'local' migrations may vary from short to moderate distances. They may be limited movements from inland breeding grounds to a more favourable feeding area near the coast. Other journeys may follow the rainy season, which encourages the growth of more blooms, fruit and seed. For, even more important than escaping the cold, birds migrate to obtain a better food supply.

The technique of bird-ringing enables experts to study the movements of migratory birds. A light-weight ring, bearing a reference and the address of the ringer, is attached to the lower leg of the bird, either when it is a young at nest, or an adult caught in a net or trap. Many millions have been ringed in recent times, mostly by dedicated amateurs. Inevitably recoveries are relatively few, but the million or so recovered bird-rings (mostly through death) provide fascinating knowledge about bird migration.

The Arctic Tern is the greatest traveller of all. It regularly covers 10,000 miles (16,000 km.) during the late summer, voyaging from its northern colonies to the seas in the south near Antarctica. The most spectacular migrant in Europe is the White Stork. To reach

Opposite: Its appearance clearly indicates the origin of the African Spoonbill's name.

Right: The Greenshank is recorded in large numbers at the coast.

Right: The Little Stint, in its non-breeding winter plumage, is a very common wader found all over Kenya in aquatic habitats.

its wintering ground in South Africa, a bird from Denmark has to make a journey of 8,000 miles (13,000 km.).

The speed of travel for most small birds is around 30 miles (50 km.) per hour. Migrating hawks cruise at about 40 miles (65 km.), shorebirds or waders average 50 miles (80 km.) and ducks nearer 60 miles (96 km.) per hour. At such speeds migrating birds may cover hundreds of miles in a day or night, and routinely fly non-stop for 500 miles (800 km.). A Turnstone ringed in Germany travelled 510 miles (820 km.) in 25 hours. Blue Geese have been known to journey 1,700 miles (2,750 km.) in 60 hours.

How do birds navigate their way over such vast distances with relative ease? Even with the great deal of knowledge now at hand, the complete answer is still shrouded in mystery but there are specialist books on the subject.

It is estimated that Africa south of the Sahara supports as many as 3,750 billion migrants a year. Hundreds of millions more fail to complete their hazardous journeys south, destroyed by natural catastrophes. Exact figures are almost impossible to find, but in 1904 three quarters of a million migrating Longspurs were found dead in an area of 2 square miles (5.2 sq. km.) in Iowa following a sudden snowstorm.

The whole of Europe, Africa north of the Sahara, and Asia north of the Himalayas, together form a zoogeographical zone known as the Palaearctic Region. And it is from this vast area that migrants winter regularly in some part of Africa south of the Sahara. East Africa as a whole receives 159 species, about 29 of which are waders or shorebirds. The remainder include warblers, shrikes, ducks, falcons, gulls and others.

A visitor from Europe familiar with waders in his home country may yet find the migrant waders in Africa difficult to identify. This is because in many species the summer, or breeding, plumage differs considerably from that of the winter. The latter is somewhat drab while the former is more elaborate and colourful, designed to attract the opposite sex during the mating season. The problem of identification becomes even more complex during April–May when some waders begin to change into their summer plumage in anticipation of flights back to their breeding grounds in the north.

While the **Greenshank** is a common migrant to all wetlands habitats in Kenya, the largest numbers are recorded from the coast. Being 12 in. (30 cm.) long, it is a sizeable wader, with a slightly up-curved bill. Its widespread breeding area extends from Scotland across Europe to Siberia.

The **Little Stint**, is only 5 in. (12.5 cm.) in size and so the smallest of the wintering shorebirds. It has already arrived by the beginning of August, having left its breeding grounds in the USSR (birds ringed at the Rift Valley lakes have also been recovered there), making its way along the eastern Mediterranean.

A small dumpy bird, seemingly always in a hurry, running at breakneck speed as it feeds along the tide edge, is the **Sanderling**. It has a highly disrupted breeding range, the main areas being in eastern Greenland, and parts of Siberia and Arctic America. Apparently some of the population which leaves the Arctic to winter in Africa uses Britain and other North Sea coasts as staging posts to fatten up before moving further south. More waders or

Left: The wader one may see running rapidly to and fro as it feeds along the tide edge is undoubtedly the Sanderling.

Left: The Water Thicknee is nocturnal and is generally found in the vicinity of water.

Opposite: The Carmine Bee-eater is very gregarious and roosts in large numbers on mangrove islands at the coast.

shorebirds, also to be seen at the coast, are referred to elsewhere in this book.

Besides the tidal seashore, the coast provides a number of other wet habitats, which may be favoured by certain species, including the Little Stints, Sanderlings and Marsh Sandpipers already mentioned. These areas include creeks, narrow recesses in the shore subject to tidal movements; estuaries, where the current at the mouth of a river meets the sea's tides and is subject to their effects; and salt pans, which are small basins or depressions flooded by salt deposits. Tidal creeks are often lined with mangroves, which may also form dense swamps. Mangroves are mostly low trees or shrubs growing in shore mud with many tangled roots above ground.

Among the birds found in these localities, the **Great White Egret**, almost 36 in. (90 cm) long with striking all-white plumage, has entirely black legs and a noticeably long black or yellow bill. A member of the heron family, it can be readily distinguished from its close relatives, the Yellow-billed Egret and the Little Egret, by these characteristics.

Locally seen at coastal salt pans, estuaries and creeks is another similar sized bird with all-white plumage but here its resemblance to the previous species ends. It has bare red legs and face. This is the **African Spoonbill** and why it is so called is clear from its long, spatulate bill shaped somewhat like a spoon.

In lagoons and estuaries you may also come across the **Sacred Ibis**. With its white feathers, bare black head and neck, and down-curved elongated bill, this distinctive ibis was regarded as sacred by the ancient Egyptians. It was revered as the embodiment of Thoth, the god of wisdom, who was depicted with the head of an ibis on many murals and tombs. But the Sacred Ibis has been extinct in Egypt for well over a hundred years.

A strange-looking bird, about 14 in. (35 cm.) long, with a large head and big yellow eyes, the **Water Thicknee** is widespread along the creeks and islands. The large eyes are an adaptation for its mainly nocturnal habits. In some respects thicknees resemble bustards, but in others they are more like plovers. They are, however, a family in their own right.

It stands to reason that a bird of prey which feeds largely on fish must also make its home at the coast. This is indeed so. In the calm waters of creeks and estuaries a **Fish Eagle** can find plenty to suit its diet. This species is widespread in Kenya, wherever suitable water is found, and has already been mentioned.

Some species of kingfishers are fish-eaters, others live, often far from water, mainly on insects, and the remainder have a mixed diet. The **Pied Kingfisher**, which is a distinctive black-and-white bird, can be seen in its characteristic hovering flight over waters of creeks and estuaries. Immediately its prey is spotted, the bird plunges headlong into the water with eyes closed and comes up immediately, with or without the fish. Its chances of a successful catch are only about one in ten.

A great deal of the shoreline at the coast is thickly wooded and when the indigenous trees in the forest are in fruit, one is often attracted by loud raucous brayings and grunts along its edge. These could well originate from a **Silvery-cheeked Hornbill**. About

Above: Of the nineteen species of pigeons and doves to be seen in Kenya, the Speckled Pigeon is the largest.

Left: The Little Bee-eater, like its allied species, has developed a remarkable technique of de-stinging captured bees.

Above: The big casque on the Silvery-cheeked Hornbill is extremely light, the interior being porous bony tissue.

Right: At lower altitudes, near water, the Golden Palm Weavers are a hive of industry, building their woven nests.

28 in. (70 cm.) in size, it belongs to a distinctive group of birds with an unusually big down-curved bill, frequently surmounted by a large, often grotesque, growth on the upper mandible. Contrary to what you might expect, this casque is extremely light, being filled with spongy bone tissue.

As you move inland from the sea, the bushy grassland has its own attractive birdlife. Slim birds, with long slightly down-curved bills and brilliant plumage, fly gracefully from tree or bush perches hawking for bees and similar insects. These are bee-eaters. The most eye-catching is the **Carmine Bee-eater** 14 in. (35 cm.) long, with its very elongated central tail feather. As the name implies, it is mostly carmine-red, with greenish and cobalt-blue head, neck and rump. They breed in the Lake Turkana basin in the north and travel to the lowlands and coast between November and the end of March when they are sometimes seen in their thousands roosting in mangroves north of Mombasa.

The **Little Bee-Eater** offers a sharp contrast to the above, being 6 in. (15 cm.) in length, mostly green, with a yellow throat, and lacking the elongated tail feather.

Along the course of a coastal river or stream, in trees, bushes and reeds, can be seen and heard a noisy chattering breeding-colony of an entirely yellow bird, 6 in. (15 cm.) in size, with a bright orange head and a black eye. This is the **Golden Palm Weaver** frequently associated with its look-alike, the Golden Weaver which, however, has a chestnut head and pale red eye. Weavers and their nests form an interesting topic for Chapter 5.

Woodlands: open, acacia and others

The habitats described in the first three chapters essentially lack any vegetational significance and, being so highly specialized, their bird communities have been somewhat easy to define. Beginning with this chapter we now enter areas which spread throughout the country at varying altitudes and, consequently, where the bird species present show much variation. The headings of the last four chapters are to a certain extent arbitrary, and differentiated mainly for convenience.

The word 'woodland' is self-descriptive and at its simplest means land covered with trees. If their growth is extensive it becomes a forest. A good example of a dense acacia woodland is the area surrounding the main track which leads from the entrance towards the lake in the Nakuru National Park. At its periphery the trees thin out to become open woodland with acacia dotted among grassy areas. In Nairobi National Park a similar habitat is found at the Hippo Pools, with the added bonus of a meandering river. Much of the land surrounding Lake Naivasha is also rewarding open woodland.

The **Secretary Bird**, sole member of its family, is found exclusively in Africa. It is usually seen in pairs from sea level to 10,000 ft. (3,000 m.) in bushed grassland and open plains. It is a terrestrial bird of prey, and, full-grown, stands over 36 in. (90 cm.) in height with a wingspan of 7 ft. (2.1 m.). Its grey and black plumage, long legs with black 'plus-fours', elongated central tail feathers and the conspicuous crest, which can be raised like a halo, makes it readily recognizable.

Below: The Secretary Bird owes its name partly to the remarkable crest of elongated feathers protruding from the head, reminiscent of quill pens of olden days stuck behind a secretary's ear.

Opposite: The Augur Buzzard is frequently seen along Kenya roads, perched on telegraph posts.

Most of its life is spent on the ground, walking with graceful strides, looking for its prey of insects, rats and particularly snakes. It wages incessant war on the latter, killing the snake by pounding it on the ground with sledgehammer blows of the feet. The bird performs extraordinary somersaults and contortions, with its wings outstretched as a protective measure, to avoid getting poisonous bites while carrying out this operation. It is undoubtedly of great economic value because of its destruction of vermin.

The most frequently seen bird of prey in Kenya must be the **Augur Buzzard**. A particularly distinctive thing about this hawk is its choice of a high vantage point on which to sit for long periods gazing over the territory to scout out its prey. Any perch will do, the branch of a tree, a high rock, or even a telegraph post. And it is on these that the traveller, as he drives along the Kenya roads, spots the Augur Buzzard.

The bird is readily recognized by its slaty-grey upper parts and its generally entirely white underparts. Confusion in identification may be caused by the fact that about ten per cent of them are melanistic, which means having dark or black pigment granules in their feathers, so that the underpart, instead of being entirely white, may be black on the throat and chest, or even completely black. But the one diagnostic feature, clearly visible when the bird is in flight, is its chestnut coloured tail.

Found at heights between 1,300–15,000 ft. (400–4,600 m.), the augur buzzard's main diet consists of ground-living rodents, reptiles and insects and thus it can be regarded as useful to man.

The term 'game-bird' is loosely used nowadays in various parts of the world to describe birds caught or killed for eating. In Kenya, these birds are now subject to game laws and can only be shot under licence. The law is designed to protect them from excessive human predation and their capture and killing is strongly controlled by issuing limited licences during specific times of the year.

There was a time not long ago when the **Helmeted Guinea-fowl** could be seen in flocks numbering as many as 2,000. But, alas, in recent years they have been killed extensively for the pot, and perhaps their last stronghold is in the Masai areas.

An attractive large bird, about 22 in. (55 cm.) in size, it is generally black and spotted thickly all over with white. A bony crest or horn protrudes from the crown of its head. Awakening early at first light with a vociferous dawn chorus, they make their leisurely way to water, eating their diet of insects, seeds and roots as they go.

The mention of pigeons brings to mind the image of large flocks in many towns throughout the world such as Trafalgar Square in London or outside St. Mark's Church in Venice. These are the wild descendents of the many breeds of domestic pigeon, whose

Below: The Helmeted Guineafowl is another game bird. It is often seen in flocks, but these no longer number up to 2,000 as they frequently did in the past.

Right : Of the five species of rollers seen in Kenya the resident Lilac-breasted Roller is the most handsome.

Right : This turkey-like bird is the Ground Hornbill, the largest member of its family. It generally forages for food on the ground.

ancestor is the Rock Pigeon. Although once domesticated, perhaps as a source of food, in big cities today the large feral flocks have become a pest and, in some countries, they have been poisoned or shot in large numbers. More humane methods are now being tried, but the problem is far from solved.

There are around 300 species of pigeons worldwide in temperate and tropical areas of the world. Kenya has 16, of which the **Speckled Pigeon** at 16 in. (40 cm.) is the largest. It is very widespread, being found between 1,600–10,000 ft. (500–3,000 m.) in acacia woodlands, on cliffs, and even associated with human habitations. It is readily identified, with its brownish back and wings (the latter with white spots), grey underparts, and marked 'dominoes' round its eye.

Most owls hunt at night and can therefore be regarded as nocturnal counterparts of birds of prey which hunt for food in daytime, but the two groups are not closely related. All owls are distinctive with their big round heads set on the body, apparently without a neck, and the unusual facial disc in which both eyes are directed forward.

The owl has developed a number of features as a consequence of its nocturnal habits, which makes it a very efficient hunter. The large size of its two eyes is designed to gather as much light as possible, and although each has a relatively small field of view, the two areas overlap almost completely, thus giving the bird excellent binocular vision, which enables it to judge distances accurately. The owl can turn its head almost right round, thus covering a large visual field rapidly. Its feathers are velvety soft with furry edges which act as sound-deadening devices and the flight feathers are specially adapted for silent movement. The position of the auditory ears (in no way connected to the external 'ears') and their structure make for very acute hearing and the bird can locate exactly the origin and direction of any sound.

The **Verraux's Eagle Owl** is a reasonably common resident of woodland, and conspicuous because of its large size (24 in., 60 cm.). When its eyes are closed, the upper lid is noticeably pink.

The classified order to which such attractive families as kingfishers, bee-eaters, hoopoes and hornbills belong also contains the family of rollers, and these must run the kingfishers a close second in beauty. The **Lilac-breasted Roller** is perhaps the most eye-catching of all.

Tawny-brown on top, rich lilac on the throat and breast, with the remaining plumage of various shades of bright blue and greenish-blue, these birds carry out brilliant aerobatics during their courtship displays when they somersault and roll spectacularly. This accounts for their name. They perch on high vantage points, natural or artificial, from which to make sorties to catch a

Below: The Nubian Woodpecker has a strong, straight bill enabling it to chisel a nest hole with amazing rapidity.

Opposite: The Paradise Flycatcher is the most beautiful of all flycatchers, particularly the male with its elongated tail feathers, later lost in moult.

large insect or lizard; and a grass fire, with its escaping insects, is a particular attraction for them.

The most prominent and distinctive feature of hornbills is the unusually large, generally down-curved bill which is often surmounted by a large casque. The exaggerated mandibles and the casque give the impression of a top-heavy bird liable to tip over its head, but these appendages are extremely light, having a horny shell filled with a supporting network of loose, delicate and spongelike bone tissue. Some authorities think the casques act as resonance chambers for the bird's call.

The **Ground Hornbill** is the largest member of the family, being 42 in. (103 cm.) in size. It resembles a domestic turkey in appearance, but not in taste! The plumage is generally black and the skin of its face and throat is red in the male and usually blue in the female. They are often seen in open savannah country in family parties of two to eight, quartering their territory on foot, looking for food, which may consist of fruit and berries, insects, small mammals, reptiles and even birds. Nests are made in hollow trees and, occasionally, in small caves in a cliff face.

The woodpecker derives its name from its habit of climbing up trees and drilling into the bark for insect prey, a technique which is highly developed in the family. The **Nubian Woodpecker**, often seen at Naivasha, is typical.

Its legs are short, with strong feet and the tail is wedge-shaped and stiff. These specialized structures form a three-point contact to facilitate tree climbing. The extraordinarily long tongue with its mucous-coating can be protruded extremely to catch ants, lick sap from trees, or as a lance to spear large insects. The bill is strong, straight and chisel-like and used both for 'drumming' by rapid blows to bore into wood for larvae and for excavating nest holes at an astounding rate.

There are many members in the large flycatcher family. These are medium sized birds which generally perch on a suitable branch and make erratic sorties to catch insects on the wing.

The male **Paradise Flycatcher** must be the most colourful. With its combination of glossy-black chest, neck and head, blue eye-ring and bill, and black flight feathers, it is unmistakable. In some areas, particularly along the coast, it is more common in its white phase, when the tail, back and wings are white.

The nest is a small neat cup in the fork of a tree, built of twigs, grass and lichen. Cobwebs are used in its construction and also to help anchor it firmly to the branch. It is somewhat absurd to see an adult male overhanging its tiny nest. Another member of the family commonly seen in gardens is the attractive **White-eyed Slaty Flycatcher**. As it alights on the ground to pick up insects, it is a symphony in tones of grey, with a conspicuous white eye-ring.

Above: Only when the Blue-eared Glossy Starling catches the sun is its multi-coloured iridescence seen at its best.

Left: The White-eyed Slaty Flycatcher is an elegant bird, with its varied grey plumage. It catches insects on the wing in characteristic fashion.

Below: The White-headed Buffalo Weaver is conspicuous in flight as it flashes its orange-red rump and under-tail feathers.

Starlings are perhaps the commonest birds in Europe, where they live in close proximity to human habitation whose residents are accustomed to ignoring this rather nondescript bird with its speckled plumage. So it comes as a startling surprise to see the colourful starlings of Africa.

Although seen less frequently than the more common Superb Starling, the **Blue-eared Glossy Starling** is a rewarding spectacle in bright sunlight. The metallic iridescent colours appear green, but occasionally bluish, violet or even golden in certain lights. The orange-yellow eye is characteristic.

Travelling through wooded grassland below 4,500 ft. (1,400 m.), you often see a bird, with a white head and a conspicuously red rump, in flight. This is the **White-headed Buffalo Weaver**. It seems to have no association with the buffalo in spite of its name. It is catholic in taste, eating seeds, fruit and insects. The nest, hung from the branch of a thorn tree, is an untidy retort-like structure, with an entrance from below. It is made of thorny twigs for protection, and lined with grass or feathers.

Semi-arid and arid bush and scrub

In those areas of Kenya where the rainfall is less than 12 in. (30 cm.), grass cover is erratic, being at its maximum after the rains, but soon disappearing, leaving denuded and barren ground. Dwarf bushes and scrub are often present, but desert and semi-desert conditions prevail.

The east and south-east areas of Lake Turkana are typical of such habitats. These arid areas at first sight seem unlikely habitats for birds, but they have a great abundance of birdlife and are rewarding to visit.

The **Pale Chanting Goshawk** is a member of the goshawk family and is generally a resident of dry-bush and semi-desert country. The chanting goshawks have acquired the name because of the melodious call repeated for hours on end during the early breeding season. The chant is also made on the wing and the pair display by soaring together in circles about 200–300 ft. (60–90 m.) above the ground.

It is a very upright pale grey hawk, 19 in. (48 cm.) long with bright reddish-orange legs, finely-barred belly and a white rump, which is conspicuous in flight. Unlike other hawks, it spends considerable time on the ground walking about with ease and even running fast to pursue prey. Its main diet consists of lizards, but it will also eat frogs, small snakes, grasshoppers and other insects.

Of medium to large size, bustards are well suited to their life in deserts and bushy plains, their strong legs being adapted to their

Left: The Pale Chanting Goshawk has acquired its name because of its melodious call, repeated for hours on end during the breeding season.

Left: The ornamental feathers on the neck of the Kori Bustard are used in remarkable mating displays.

Opposite: The Spotted Thicknee, usually seen on dry land, has large eyes, characteristic of nocturnal birds.

terrestrial habits. The **Kori Bustard** is the biggest member of the family living in Kenya and is around 40 in. (100 cm.) long. It is best identified by its large size. The wings are broad, and its flight, though laboured, is powerful and rapid. Ornamental plumes occur on head, nape and long neck in the form of loose feathers which are used in remarkable breeding displays. When threatened they hide by crouching low. The birds are omnivorous and will take animal and vegetable matter.

The **Spotted Thicknee**, previously known as the Spotted Stone Curlew, is the dry country counterpart of the Water Thicknee already mentioned in Chapter 3. It is somewhat larger than the latter, and has the same big eyes adapted to its nocturnal habits. Thicknees are habitually watchful and spend the day in the shade standing or sitting still. Although their cryptic appearance enables them to virtually disappear into their surroundings, when approached they will flatten themselves on the ground with head and neck outstretched. At night they become quite active and noisy, especially during the breeding season.

The sandgrouse family has a closer affinity to pigeons than to any other family. They also resemble pigeons in size, but their colouring matches the arid area in which they live, making it possible for them to nest out in the open, generally near a bush. Their diet is entirely vegetarian, consisting mainly of various grasses and seeds.

Because of the hot, dry conditions in which they are resident, and their diet of grain, sandgrouse have a need to drink at least once a day and sometimes twice, and this need becomes even greater when the young are hatched. These can feed themselves almost immediately, but must rely on the parent for their water supply.

Flights often cover up to 50 miles (80 km.) to the source of water either at dawn or near sunset. Naturally gregarious, the birds gather in flocks before flying and are joined by more on the way, ending up in flocks of hundreds or even thousands. With a cruising speed of around 40–50 miles (65–80 km.) an hour, the journey takes about an hour. They descend directly – and rapidly – when they reach the water, quench their thirst within 20 or 30 seconds, and are ready to leave immediately. This rapid turnaround is a mechanism to decrease their vulnerability to predation brought about by their large numbers.

Those males who have young chicks to satisfy crouch down in the water and thoroughly soak their belly feathers. They then make a long, slower journey back to the nest area where the young are being looked after by the female. The male stands upright with its feathers fluffed out, the chicks crouch beneath him and draw the water out of his plumage with their beaks. It has been scientifically confirmed that their specially evolved belly feathers hold three times as much water as those of other birds, and maintain their structure in spite of the regular wetting and sucking. These

Above: The call of the Laughing Dove explains why it is so named.

Left: The Chestnut-bellied Sandgrouse will make regular flights of as much as 50 miles (80 km.) to obtain water for its young.

Below: Occasionally seen raiding chicken farms,
Verraux's Eagle Owl has distinctive pink upper
eyelids noticeable when it closes its eye.

feathers in the female are not so effectively developed.

The **Chestnut-bellied Sandgrouse** is the most common species of the family in Kenya, where it inhabits arid bush country and plains.

The only difference between pigeons and doves is that of size, the former being appreciably larger. The **Laughing Dove** is only about 9 in. (23 cm.) in size and is therefore just over half the size of the Speckled Pigeon mentioned in the previous chapter. Its name is derived from its distinctive five note call which, with some imagination, may sound like a laugh.

It is common knowledge that pigeons feed their young with their 'milk', but this is not a secretion of the mammary glands. For the first few days the chicks are fed exclusively on 'pigeon's milk', which is an emulsion made from the cells of the lining and the oil globules from the fatty layers of the crop. The diet is then augmented gradually by seeds and fruit until the young achieve the adult diet of mostly berries, seeds and buds.

Besides the down–curved bill surmounted by a casque mentioned previously (see Chapter 4), the hornbill family has another important distinction. In the 1960s Joan and Alan Root produced their fascinating nature film *The Baobab Tree*, which featured a complete and intimate sequence of the nesting of a pair of **Red-billed Hornbills** at Tsavo National Park, photographed through a window cut into the back of the nest.

This astounding film, and research carried out by other workers, have given us a complete picture of the breeding process of the hornbill. To start with, the female Red-billed Hornbill finds a suitable hole or hollow in a tree and proceeds to wall herself in. The male supplies the material, mainly mud, dung and saliva, and this is regurgitated to the female in the form of pellets. These are patted into the entrance hole until the opening is reduced to a narrow vertical slit. The female can no longer leave the nest and settles down to lay three to six eggs, the male continuing to feed her through the small opening.

During incubation the female moults. As the eggs hatch and the chicks grow, the male works hard to feed the vociferous and demanding family until the female grows new feathers and breaks out, though the young are still half-grown. The chicks have the ability to repair the damaged exit by re-plastering as soon as the mother has left. Now both parents feed the hungry brood until the young are fully grown and break out of the nest with the adults' help.

Those who visit the dry country surrounding the strongly alkaline Lake Magadi (see Chapter 2), can hear a remarkable and unmistakable birdsong which, in fact, is a duet, sometimes even a chorus. Variously described, sometimes as 'toogle-de-doogle' repeated over and over again, it is the call of the **Red and Yellow Barbets**. Those fortunate enough to see the birds duetting, will

Below: The Red-billed Hornbill nests in natural holes in trees, the opening being almost completely walled up by the female to leave only a narrow slit through which the male feeds her.

Above: The Red and Yellow Barbets perform a fascinating display in the form of a song and dance duet.

Right: The most frequently seen of the starlings is the Superb Starling and it certainly lives up to its name.

observe that they 'seem to work themselves up into a great state of excitement and perform many curious antics' as recorded by Sir Frederick Jackson in his *Birds of Kenya Colony and the Uganda Protectorate*.

Barbets are primarily forest birds, but a few, like the Red and Yellow Barbet, have adapted to live in semi-arid areas.

The **Superb Starling**, one of the commonest and most photographed birds in Kenya, is readily recognized by its metallic greenish-blue back, black head, and narrow white band across the breast separating the metallic-blue upper parts from the bright chestnut belly. It is noisy, conspicuous and gregarious and commonly seen feeding on the ground in small parties. The nest generally consists of a ball of grass with a tunnel entrance at the side, surrounded by thorny twigs.

East Africa has the second largest family of weavers, boasting 89 members out of a world total of 142 species. They are aptly named because they all share the ability to tie a knot and so build a truly woven nest, which is completely enclosed.

Weavers start their nests by taking a long piece of grass, which they usually place at the tip of a branch, holding one end down with a claw and then, with the beak, proceeding to work the other end in, out and over, thus fastening it as a knot. This procedure is continued until a suspended ring is formed, providing the basis of the nest. More and more strands are woven in, the bird standing in the middle of the ring, until a hollow ball is made. Each piece of grass is meticulously worked in, the end pulled through and the loose end tucked away.

The **Vitelline Masked Weaver** builds an elaborate hanging nest, with the entrance at the bottom. A safety partition is provided to prevent the eggs from falling out. Its suspension from the end of a slim branch is another safety device against predation by monkeys, snakes etc. Some weavers build even more elaborate nests, access being gained through a long entrance tunnel hanging down vertically at the side. Other survival measures include building nests very close to homes of stinging insects, large birds or even human beings.

One very common bird, seen and heard while on safari in dry country when hardly daylight, starts up a tuneless 'chuk chuk' call and various loud monotonous chatterings. Their appearance is equally nondescript, but attractive in a muted way. They are **White-browed Sparrow Weavers**, whose rather loose and untidy nests can readily be seen on the surrounding acacia trees.

Below: White-browed Sparrow Weavers are gregarious and noisily conspicuous in dry bush and acacia country.
Opposite: The first sign of rain triggers the Vitelline Masked Weaver into weaving its nest.

Grasslands: open, bushed and wooded

Only 20 miles (32 km.) from Nairobi is situated the small township of Athi River, named after the river which flows through it. From there the vast Athi Plains roll away in all directions as far as the eye can see.

After the rains the plains are lush and green, and gazelle, wildebeeste and zebra feast on the abundant grass, and breed. Waterholes abound. As the weather becomes drier and the vegetation dies back, the animals with their young make their way back to the grasslands of the Nairobi National Park where man-made dams provide water all year round. The predators follow and the cycle of nature continues.

The luxuriant vegetation produces flowers which attract insects; the dry grass grows seed, and a multitude of birds are drawn to the nourishment so provided. It is in such surroundings that one may see the majestic **Ostrich**. The adult male stands nearly 8 ft. (2.4 m.) and weighs over 300 lbs. (136 kg.). It is the only living representative of its family and is confined exclusively to Africa. The two sexes are easy to tell apart as a male has black plumage, and the female is greyish-brown.

The Ostrich cannot fly, but its powerful legs are well evolved for efficient running. It can maintain a steady speed of about 29 miles (48 km.) an hour for almost half an hour, and produce brief bursts of speed of up to 40 miles (64 km.) an hour if necessary. The wings are often used for energetic and spectacular displays.

The male is polygamous and may consort with three to five hens. Eggs are laid by all the hens in the same hollow in the ground at the rate of one every other day up to eight eggs. So the nest may contain anything between 20–40 eggs. Incubation is about 40 days and is carried out mainly by the cock, but the dominant hen takes over for some of the daylight hours. A large proportion of the clutch fails to hatch, partly because of predation, but mainly because the sitting bird cannot cover all the eggs. Young birds become active immediately after hatching and are shepherded by the cock and the dominant hen. The pair continue to escort the chicks for a considerable time until almost fully grown.

When travelling through the plains where wild or domestic animals graze, a familiar sight are the flocks of largish mainly white birds associated with them. They prey on insects disturbed by the movement of the herds. The birds are **Cattle Egrets**, one of the few species which has benefitted from the presence of man. The introduction of domestic cattle in large numbers and the consequent opening up of new areas of grassland by modern stock-farming methods, has provided the necessary ecological niche, and the Cattle Egret population has expanded explosively.

After occupying the African range in all directions, the Cattle Egret crossed the Atlantic in a westward direction, colonizing the West Indies and South America in the 1930s, and went on to establish itself in North America by the early 1950s. By 1948 it had also travelled east to Australia, and with the unexploited food supply available in these countries, the Cattle Egret continues to multiply.

The abounding plains are the happy hunting ground for Africa's

Above: A pair of Masai Ostrich, with the male on the left. Confined exclusively to Africa, they have lost their ability to fly.

Left: The Cattle Egret, frequently seen with domestic or wild animals, preys on insects disturbed by their movement.

Above: Found in all types of country, Rüppell's Vulture spends a great deal of its time circling in thermals and gliding over game country.

Right: The massive bill and bare head enables the Lappet-faced Vulture to be a very efficient carrion-eater.

big game. Members of the wild cat family roam the area questing for their daily needs. Flying high in the sky above are the scavengers looking for the remains of a kill or a carcass produced by natural causes.

The majority will be vultures of the same or allied species. They remain aloft all day circling slowly and gliding on the rising thermals. Using their keen eyesight, they observe the ground with its herds of animals and the movements of jackals and hyenas. When a corpse is spied, the vulture planes down swiftly and is soon joined by others until over a hundred of them may be present. They gorge heavily and feed to repletion, the distended crop and gizzard being able to hold over 13 lbs. (6 kg.) of food. The bloated birds find it very difficult to take off and have to retire to a secluded spot on the ground to digest their meal.

The largest African vulture, standing 40 in. (100 cm.) tall, is the **Lappet-faced Vulture**. It has a massive bill and a bald pinkish head. Rather uncommon, it can be seen most frequently in the national parks. **Ruppell's Vulture** is somewhat smaller (34 in., 85 cm.) in size, much more common, and has dark brown plumage with creamy white edges, giving it a rather spotted appearance.

The **Black-shouldered Kite** is a member of the hawk family. It is thickset, about 13 in. (32 cm.) long, pale grey above and white below, has black shoulders, a short, white, square tail and strikingly red eyes. All these unusual features combine to make it a beautiful bird of prey. It has a slow graceful flight and hovers like a kestrel. Its food consists of large insects and small mammals and a plentiful supply may attract these birds in large numbers.

Another game bird (see Helmeted Guineafowl in Chapter 4), locally plentiful, is the **Yellow-necked Spurfowl**. It frequents open bush country, particularly along the edges of forest and woodland. It is about the size of a domestic fowl, having olive-brown upperparts, with cream striations, and dark-brown under-parts, the most conspicuous feature being its yellow throat.

Like other game birds it is protected, and allowed to be killed only under stringently controlled conditions. Whereas in most countries game laws are designed to safeguard birds from excessive human predation, in the United Kingdom, curiously enough, the main purpose of their enactment seems to have been the protection of the sporting rights for the owner or occupier of the land on which the birds are found.

Plovers are usually associated with habitats which are near water, such as the sea, lakes, rivers, mudflats and swamps. The **Crowned Plover** is different. It is a resident and wanderer in grassland and bushed grassland up to 10,000 ft. (3,000 m.). With its white abdomen, pale greyish-brown upperparts, red legs, red bill with a black tip and the black head with a white ring on the crown (curiously reminiscent of a schoolboy cap), it is a handsome bird.

Like all plovers the nest is built on the ground, in a shallow indentation, quite often unlined. Both parents incubate and look after the young, which are ready to leave the nest immediately their down feathers are dry. The marking of the chicks provide excellent camouflage. On a warning call from the parent they crouch down

Left : The Yellow-necked Spurfowl, a game bird, is allowed to be shot for the pot in limited numbers in season.

Left : The Crowned Plover, which is not aquatic, has a characteristic 'school-boy' cap.

Left : A very efficient and handsome bird of prey, the Black-shouldered Kite is often seen hovering like a kestrel.

Opposite : The area between Naivasha and Nakuru in the Rift is a favoured habitat of the White-fronted Bee-eater.

while the adult bird proceeds to divert the attention of the intruder by spreading wide one of its wings and acting as if injured. This form of distraction display is common among plovers.

A bee–eater does exactly what its name suggests; it eats bees mainly, but will also take wasps, hornets and similar insects on the wing. The prey is generally caught in the course of short flights made from a perch. Although the birds have a high immunity to bee venom, it is necessary for them to use a special technique to catch such dangerous insects. The bee is caught between the two mandibles at the tip of the bill while in flight. Back on the perch, the bee–eater expertly changes its grip so that the bee is now held near the end of the abdomen where the sting is. The head is knocked vigorously against a branch a number of times until all the venom is discharged. Two more raps on the head and the now harmless bee is ready to swallow.

The **White-fronted Bee-eater**, like other members of the family, is a fearless, slim bird, readily identified by its brilliantly coloured plumage. It breeds in colonies which often number hundreds. Tunnels are dug almost horizontally in the walls of a bank or in crevices extending to as much as 7 ft. (2.1 m.), the end being expanded into an oval nesting chamber.

Larks are ground–living, usually quietly coloured birds and their main claim to fame is their exquisite song which serves both for courtship and territorial defence. They generally pour out their song from a perch on a post or even a small eminence such as a stone. Larks prefer open country and a drive through bushed grassland early in the morning can produce a bird on every suitable perch singing its heart out. The **Red-winged Bush Lark** illustrated in this book is typical. As may be expected, all larks make their nests on the ground, sometimes a mere scraping lined with grass.

Larks and pipits predominate on the open grasslands of Africa, and although somewhat alike in appearance, the two families are not closely related. The family of pipits consists of graceful and slender birds, with an upright stance. The **Rosy-breasted Longclaw** is a sturdy pipit with streaky-brown upper parts, bright salmon-red underparts and a black chest band. I was fortunate enough to visit Nairobi National Park one day where suddenly the grassy plains were alive with flame-coloured birds, flying from one low bush to the next, disappearing in the long grass and then reappearing somewhere else. It was richly rewarding.

Rhinoceros, giraffe, zebra, buffalo, various antelope, even wart-hog, and most domestic stock are visited by two closely related species of birds which obtain their entire food supply from the hides of animals, both wild and domestic. These are oxpeckers, also known as tick-birds because of their feeding behaviour. It comes as something of a surprise to find that they belong to the family of starlings.

Taking the **Red-billed Oxpecker** as an example, the bird walks about on the animal in the manner of a woodpecker, its structural peculiarities, especially the stiffened tail and the sharp, curved claws, enabling it to maintain its hold and move about in any

Top left : From the rear the Rosy-breasted Longclaw is quite nondescript ; the bright salmon-red throat and breast come as a surprise when it is viewed from the front.

Left : The somewhat nondescriptly coloured Red-winged Bush Lark, has an exquisite song, like the other members of its family.

Opposite right: The male Red-naped Widowbird only develops its red nape and elongated tail feathers during the breeding season.

Above: Both domestic and wild animals are sometimes seen with birds on them, usually Red-billed Oxpeckers like these.

direction on the animal without difficulty. Its main nourishment comes from engorged ticks, but flies, scar tissue, blood and living tissue, and the discharge from open wounds on the 'hosts' are also taken. Thus the damage caused to the hide of domestic animals makes the bird unpopular with cattle breeders.

A member of the weaver family, the **Red-naped Widowbird** male, in its striking breeding plumage, has an entirely black body with a scarlet crown and nape. The elongated tail feathers developed at this time make it 11 in. (27 cm.) long. The female is only 5 in. (12 cm.) in size, much less colourful, being nondescript tawny and buff, and is difficult to tell from females of allied species. The breeding season over, the male moults and loses its handsome tail feathers and the scarlet colouring. The new feathers are like those of the female and the once attractive male is no longer distinguishable until the next breeding season.

Highlands: in and around Nairobi

Nairobi qualifies for a habitat chapter on its own for a number of reasons. Many visitors to Kenya arrive here first. Well-tended gardens with their flowers, shrubs, creepers and trees provide nectar, fruit and seed for food, and green lawns are a home for worms and insects. All these, combined with the varied environment, make it an area with great bird potential.

Flying over Nairobi and its environs it is surprising to see how the city and its suburbs have developed on a series of ridges and valleys, the latter with slowly running streams with varying amounts of water. Birds which rely on water for their food supply find the trees bordering these watercourses attractive and one of them is the **Hamerkop**.

The Hamerkop is the sole species of its family and has a wide range in tropical Africa. It is a sombre and heavy-looking bird of medium size (20 in., 50 cm.) with brown plumage. Its conspicuous feature is a long backward-pointing crest, looking somewhat like a hammer, which gives rise to its name. Its nest is a remarkable structure built of sticks and other vegetation, lined with mud or dung, in the fork of a tree near a river or swamp. It is enormous in size, being up to 3–4 ft. (90–100 cm.) in diameter, with a side entrance leading to an enclosed chamber. Birds tend to return to the old nest and add to it in successive years, causing the structure to collapse eventually under its sheer weight. The food of hamerkops consists mainly of frogs and tadpoles, caught from a perch, sometimes even from the back of a hippopotamus.

Who has not seen members of the kite family, in their thousands,

Below: The Hamerkop or Hammerhead, so called because of the shape of its head.

Opposite: The Red-eyed Dove is one of three doves which have a black half-collar on the back of the neck.

Opposite bottom: The Black Kite is a common scavenger, seen regularly around towns and villages.

scavenging in the towns and villages of Europe, Asia and Africa? Of them the **Black Kite** is one of the commonest and most obvious. This bird of prey can be seen near human habitations in Kenya up to 10,000 ft. (3,000 m) and is readily recognized by its dark brown plumage, yellow bill and markedly forked tail. Leaving Nairobi by road in the morning, you can see these birds quartering the highways for animals killed by the traffic. The kites serve a useful purpose by their scavenging of offal and dead creatures.

It is most likely that the dove you will see in Nairobi, with a half-collar on the hind-neck, will be the **Red-eyed Dove**. In size it lies between the Speckled Pigeon and the Laughing Dove already mentioned, being 12 in. (30 cm.) long. It has the typical cooing or crooning call by which all doves are distinguished. Another characteristic of the family is they way they drink, by immersing their bills in the water and sucking, instead of putting their heads up to swallow like other bird species.

There are two exceptions to the law protecting birds from hunting – the quelea and the mousebird. Both are agricultural pests as they destroy or damage grain and fruit. The Red-billed Quelea, a member of the weaver family, is entirely colonial in habit, often found in concentrations of over a million and is a menace to crops of small grain. Large-scale efforts are made to control them, but in spite of immense slaughter the plague continues.

The **Speckled Mousebird** is a member of a small family peculiar to Africa. Its body is no bigger than that of a sparrow, but it has a long tail, made up of ten stiff, graduated feathers, giving it an overall length of 13 in. (32 cm.). The head is topped by a marked crest. Altogether it is a very distinctive bird.

Mousebirds are extremely sociable and usually seen in small parties. Their feet are very strong and provided with sharp claws. The outer toes can be moved forwards or backwards. All these adaptations enable the bird to perch or cling in all kinds of positions and therefore to climb readily. Its main diet is fruit and other vegetable matter.

The **Hoopoe** is strikingly beautiful and unmistakable. It measures about 11 in. (27 cm.) from end to end and the main body plumage is bright pinkish-cinnamon. The wings and tail have alternate black and white bars. The erectile crest feathers are again pinkish with black tips, and the black bill has a slightly downward curve. They nest in a hole, either in a tree, rock, bank or even building. A pair of hoopoes can often be seen on the lawn in many gardens, hunting for their prey, which consists of large insects, their larvae, worms and lizards. Their monotonous call of 'hoop, hoop, hoop' is low and penetrating.

Looking rather like thrushes to whom they are related, the babblers move around on bushes or on the ground in noisy parties, keeping up a continuous chatter, as they search for their food, which consists mainly of insects and a little fruit. The **Northern Pied Babbler**, in recent years, has colonized gardens not only on the outskirts of Nairobi, but in the very heart of the city.

When first seen, the **Robin Chat** reminds one of the English robin. It has an orange-rufous throat and chest, a well-marked

Opposite : The attractive Speckled Mousebird is none the less a pest as it damages fruit and food crops extensively.

Right : The Hoopoe nests in any convenient hole, and even one in a building is happily accepted.

Right : In recent years Nairobi gardens have been invaded by the Northern Pied Babbler.

white eye-stripe, and a grey belly. To be awakened in the morning by the outstanding warble of this species can be delightful. In addition it is an excellent mimic of the call of other birds and, if so inclined, will give a concert of its repertoire. But it is the natural song which seems to have territorial and advertising functions. Robin Chats are rather shy, skulking birds feeding mainly on the ground, but can be relatively tame in gardens.

As shown in the illustration, the Robin Chat is often parasitized by the Red-chested Cuckoo. Briefly, this is the fascinating story. The female cuckoo keeps her potential host under close observation while the latter is nest building and sneaks in when the nest is unattended to place her egg with those of the Robin Chat, sometimes removing one laid by the latter. The cuckoo egg hatches first and the chick's instinct is to eject any other object in the nest. Thus, either the eggs or the· young of the Robin Chat are manoeuvered to the edge and pushed out, leaving the cuckoo chick in sole possession. The host parents seem to be unconcerned about their own offspring and feed the large and demanding interloper until it leaves the nest in 17–20 days. Even then, the foster parents continue to feed the growing cuckoo in the surrounding trees until about four weeks later the parasite is independent.

Most of Kenya's starlings have brilliantly coloured plumage with a metallic gloss, but perhaps the most spectacular is the male **Violet-backed Starling**, which has an iridescent purple back and head, in some lights appearing plum-coloured or even crimson, and white underparts. Unusually for this family, the female is quite different and almost dull. When the wild fig trees in Nairobi gardens come into fruit, a flock of these starlings appears out of the blue to feast themselves on the abundant figs, until three to four days later the fruit is gone and so have the birds.

Sunbirds occupy a similar niche in the warmer parts of the Old World to that filled by hummingbirds in the New World. Both groups have long curved beaks and brilliant plumage, and take nectar from flowers, thus helping in their pollination. But the two families have only superficial structural similarities and are not related.

Sunbirds are a distinct family of small birds, their length varying from 4 9 in. (10–22 cm.), with slender, pointed, down-curved bills, the male in most species having brilliantly coloured plumage, most of it with an iridescent metallic sheen. The females in most cases are drab. Their flight is rapid and rather erratic, as they move from blossom to blossom, frequently calling in their sharp metallic voices. Besides taking nectar from flowers, sunbirds eat a large quantity of small insects. Their nests are closed, with a side opening, generally made of grass or fibres, and bound together with spiders' webs.

The commonest member of the family seen in Nairobi gardens is the **Bronze Sunbird**. The male with its elongated central tail feathers is about 9 in. (22 cm.) long and shows a metallic bronzy-green iridescence in favourable light. Somewhat smaller, only 6 in. (15 cm.) in size, is the **Scarlet-chested Sunbird**. The male is rather thickset, has a square tail and near-black plumage. The head

Left : When wild fig trees are in fruit, the Violet-backed Starling is one of their most attractive visitors.

Left : Described aptly as an animated plum, the Red-billed Firefinch is often seen feeding on the ground near human dwellings.

Left : Holub's Golden Weavers build a number of nests of which only one is used. This is presumably a form of camouflage.

Opposite : The Bronze Sunbird, like other sunbirds, feeds on nectar and reminds one of American hummingbirds, but they are not related.

has a metallic green cap and the throat and chest are vivid scarlet, again only visible when the light is right. A flowerbed, with various sunbirds flitting about from blossom to blossom, forms a delightful sight.

Holub's Golden Weaver is a large weaver (8 in., 20 cm.), golden yellow in colour. The female is very similar though somewhat paler. This species is usually found in pairs, rarely in small parties, and is not gregarious. The male builds a series of large, rough and loosely woven nests, anything up to six, but only one is ever occupied.

The family of waxbills are small to very small seed-eaters and included among them is the **Red-billed Firefinch**, perhaps the most familiar bird in Africa, because of its tameness and liking for human habitations. It will wander about the garden and even on the veranda with a companion. The female is dull brown with a tinge of red on the tail, but the male plumage is entirely pinkish-red with a few whitish spots on the breast. Aptly christened an 'animated plum', this waxbill will visit the lawn, picking up minute seeds and small insects, and will readily use bird-baths. The nest, with its side entrance, is an untidy ball of dry grass, lined with feathers and usually placed low down in bushes. The bird is known to be parasitized by the Purple Indigobird, a member of the parasitic division of the vast weaver family.

Bird Index

Above: A small bird with the habits of an English robin, the Robin Chat is parasitized by the Red-chested Cuckoo.

Left: The Scarlet-chested Sunbird is almost completely black, with a vivid scarlet chest which catches the eye as it flies.

Following pages: Whistling ducks congregate on the shores of Lake Jipe, with the imposing Northern Pare Mountains in the back-ground; Sacred Ibis returning home to roost at sunset;

The Yellow-billed Stork develops a delicate pink colouration on its wings during the breeding season.